3 CHORD WORSHIP SONGS
FOR GUITAR

ISBN 978-1-4234-7935-2

HAL•LEONARD®
CORPORATION
7777 W. BLUEMOUND RD. P.O. BOX 13819 MILWAUKEE, WI 53213

Visit Hal Leonard Online at
www.halleonard.com

Agnus Dei

Words and Music by Michael W. Smith

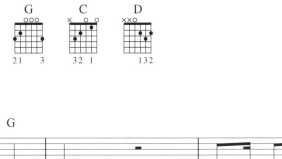

Because We Believe

Words and Music by Nancy Gordon and Jamie Harvill

Verse
Moderately fast

1. We be-lieve _ in _ God, the Fa-ther, (We be-lieve _ in _ God, the Fa-ther.)
2., 3. *See additional lyrics*

we be-lieve _ in _ Christ the Son. (We be-lieve _ in _ Christ the Son.)

We be-lieve _ in the Ho-ly Spir-it, (We be-lieve _ in the Ho-ly Spir-it.) We

are the Church _ and we stand as one. (We are the Church _ and we stand as one.)

Chorus

Ho-ly, ho-ly, ho-ly is our God. _

Wor-thy, wor-thy, wor-thy is our King. _ All

glo-ry _ and hon-or _ are His to _ re-ceive; to Je-sus _ we sing. _

1., 2. **3.**

_ be-cause we _ be-lieve.

Additional Lyrics

2. We believe in the Holy Bible, *(echo)*
   We believe in the virgin birth. *(echo)*
   We believe in the resurrection, *(echo)*
   That Christ, one day, will return to earth. *(echo)*

3. We believe in the blood of Jesus, *(echo)*
   We believe in eternal life. *(echo)*
   We believe in His love that frees us, *(echo)*
   To become the Bride of Christ. *(echo)*

Bless His Holy Name

Words and Music by Andraé Crouch

Chorus
Majestically

Bless the Lord, O my soul, and all that is with -

in me, bless His ho - ly _____ name.

Verse

He has done great things, _____ He has done great things, _____

He has done great things, bless His ho - ly name.

Chorus

Bless the Lord, O my soul, and all that is with -

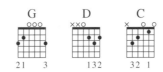

in me, bless His ho - ly _____ name.

Create in Me a Clean Heart

Words and Music by Keith Green

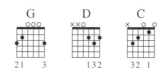

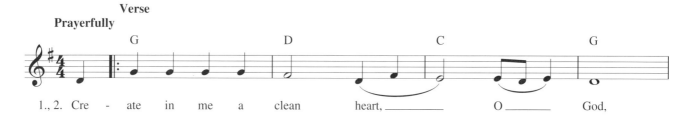

Verse
Prayerfully

1., 2. Cre - ate in me a clean heart, _____ O _____ God,

and re - new a right spir - it with - in me. 2. Cre -

Cast me not ___ a - way from Thy pres - ence, O

Lord, and take not Thy Ho - ly Spir - it from me.

Re - store un - to me the joy of Thy sal -

va - tion, and re - new a right spir - it with - in me. _____

Enough

Words and Music by Chris Tomlin and Louie Giglio

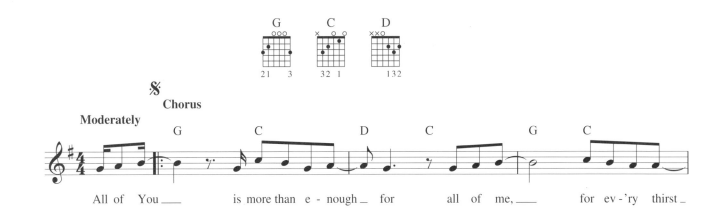

Moderately

Chorus

All of You is more than e-nough for all of me, for ev-'ry thirst and ev-'ry need. You sat-is-fy me with Your love,

To Coda

and all I have in You is more than e-nough.

Verse

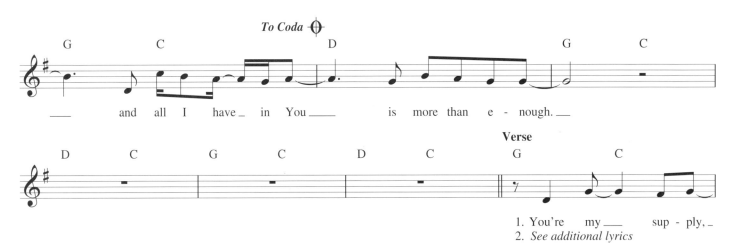

1. You're my sup-ply,
2. *See additional lyrics*

my breath of life, still more awe - some than I know.

You're my re - ward, worth liv - ing for, still more awe -

Every Move I Make

Words and Music by David Ruis

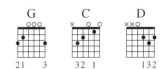

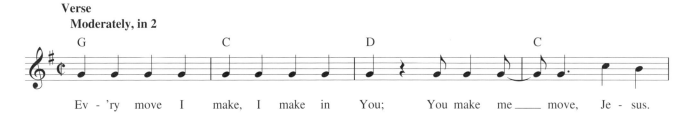

Verse
Moderately, in 2

Ev - 'ry move I make, I make in You; You make me ___ move, Je - sus.

Ev - 'ry breath I take, I breathe in You. ___

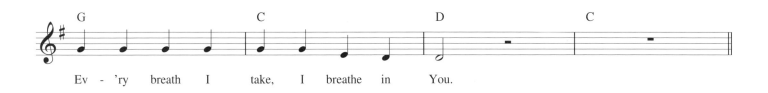

Ev - 'ry step I take, I take in You; You are my ___ way, Je - sus.

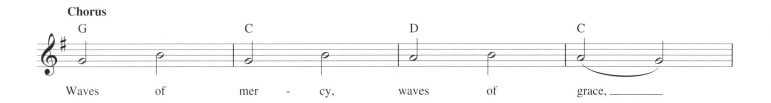

Ev - 'ry breath I take, I breathe in You.

Chorus

Waves of mer - cy, waves of grace, ___

ev - 'ry - where I look, I see _____ Your face.

Your love has cap - tured me. _____

Oh, my God, this love, how can it

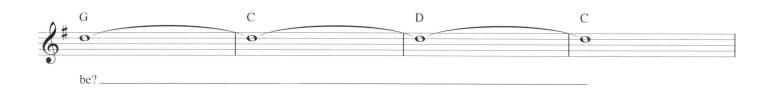

be? _____

Outro

La, la, la,

la, la, la, la. La, la, la, la, la, la, la.

Father I Adore You

Words and Music by Terrye Coelho Strom

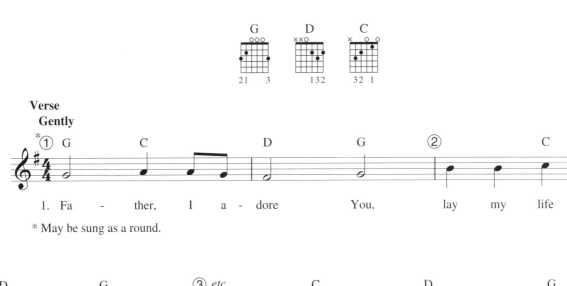

Verse
Gently

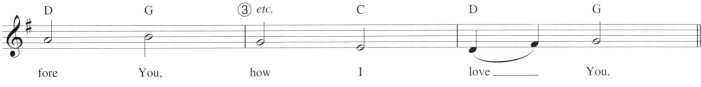

1. Fa - ther, I a - dore You, lay my life be -

* May be sung as a round.

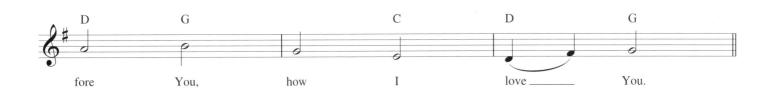

fore You, how I love _____ You.

Verse

2. Je - sus, I a - dore You, lay my life be -

fore You, how I love _____ You.

Verse

fore You, how I love _____ You.

3. Spir - it, I a - dore You, lay my life be -

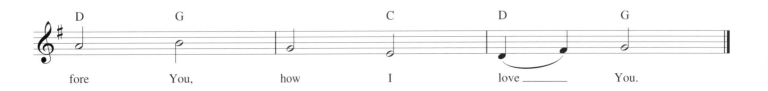

fore You, how I love _____ You.

Here I Am to Worship

Words and Music by Tim Hughes

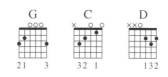

Additional Lyrics

2. King of all days, oh so highly exalted,
Glorious in heaven above.
Humbly You came to the earth You created,
All for love's sake became poor.

Holy and Anointed One

Words and Music by John Barnett

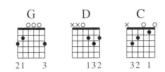

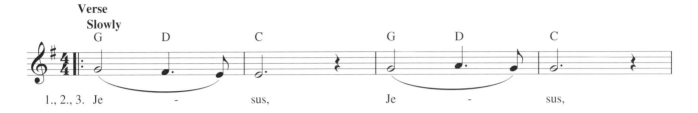

Verse
Slowly

1., 2., 3. Je - sus, Je - sus,

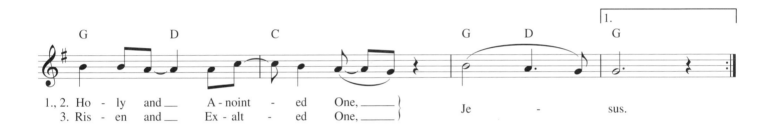

1., 2. Ho - ly and __ A - noint - ed One, ___
3. Ris - en and __ Ex - alt - ed One, ___

Je - sus.

[1.]

[2.]

%§ Bridge

sus. Your name is like hon - ey on __ my __ lips. __ Your spir - it is wa -

- ter to __ my __ soul. __ Your Word is a lamp __ un - to __ my __ feet. __

1st time, D.C.
(take 2nd ending)
2nd time, D.S. al Coda

Je - sus, I love _____ You. I love ___ You.

Coda

You. Your name is like hon - ey on ___ my ___ lips. ___ Your Spir - it is wa -

- ter to ___ my ___ soul. ___ Your Word is a lamp ___ un - to ___ my ___ feet. _

Outro-Verse

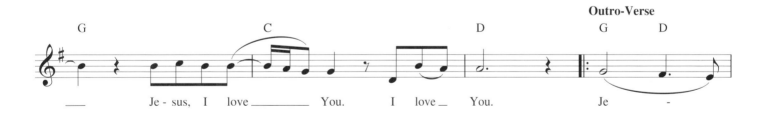

___ Je - sus, I love _____ You. I love ___ You. Je -

sus, Je - sus.

How Deep the Father's Love for Us

Words and Music by Stuart Townend

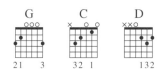

Verse

Quietly

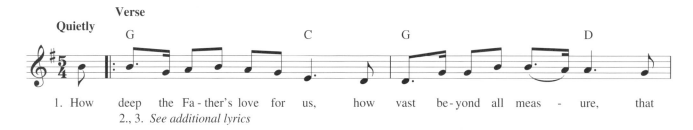

1. How deep the Fa-ther's love for us, how vast be-yond all meas - ure, that
2., 3. *See additional lyrics*

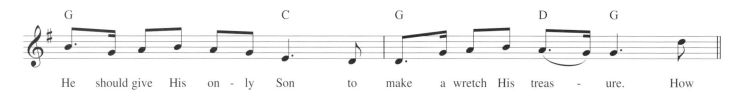

He should give His on - ly Son to make a wretch His treas - ure. How

Chorus

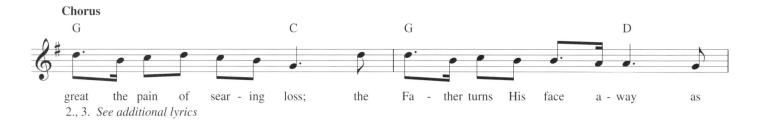

great the pain of sear - ing loss; the Fa - ther turns His face a - way as
2., 3. *See additional lyrics*

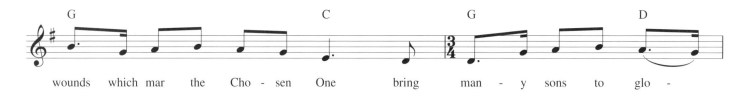

wounds which mar the Cho - sen One bring man - y sons to glo -

ry. 2. Be - som.

Additional Lyrics

2. Behold the Man upon a cross,
   My sin upon His shoulders.
   Ashamed, I hear my mocking voice
   Call out among the scoffers.

Chorus 2. It was my sin that held Him there
   Until it was accomplished;
   His dying breath has brought me life.
   I know that it is finished.

3. I will not boast in anything;
   No gifts, no pow'r, no wisdom.
   But I will boast in Jesus Christ,
   His death and resurrection.

Chorus 3. Why should I gain from His reward?
   I cannot give an answer.
   But this I know with all my heart:
   His wounds have paid my ransom.

I Could Sing of Your Love Forever

Words and Music by Martin Smith

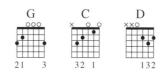

Verse
Moderately

O - ver __ the moun - tains and __ the sea   Your riv - er runs __ with love __ for me,

and I __ will o - pen up __ my heart __   and let the Heal - er set __ me free.

I'm hap - py to __ be in __ the truth   and I __ will dai - ly lift __ my hands,

Chorus

for I __ will al - ways sing __ of   when Your love came down. ___   I could sing of Your love __

__ for - ev - er.   I could sing of Your love ___ for - ev - er.

I could sing of Your love ___ for - ev - er.   I could sing of Your love __

1.   __ for - ev - er.   **2.** __ for - ev - er.

Let the River Flow

Words and Music by Darrell Patton Evans

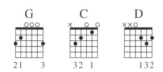

Verse

Moderately

1. Let the (2.) poor man say, "I am rich in Him," _ let the lost man say, "I am

found in Him," _ and let the riv - er flow. ___

Let the blind man say, "I can see a - gain," _ let the

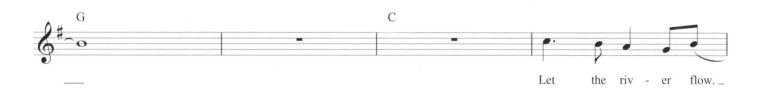

dead man say, "I am born a - gain," _ and let the riv - er flow. _

___ Let the riv - er flow. _

Chorus

Let the riv - er flow, ___

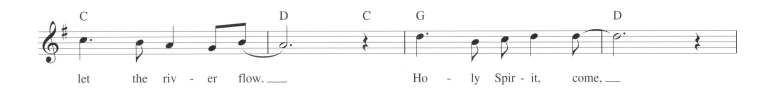

let the riv - er flow. _____ Ho - ly Spir - it, come, _____

move in pow - er. _____ Let the riv - er ___ flow. _____

2. Let the pow - er. _____ Let the riv - er ___ flow, _

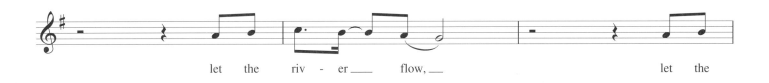

let the riv - er ___ flow, _____ let the

riv - er ___ flow, _ let the riv - er ___ flow. _____

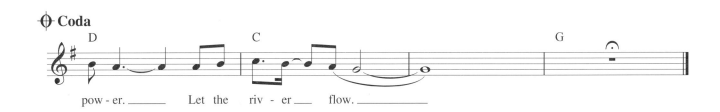

pow - er. _____ Let the riv - er ___ flow. _____

Lord I Lift Your Name on High

Words and Music by Rick Founds

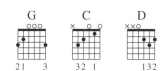

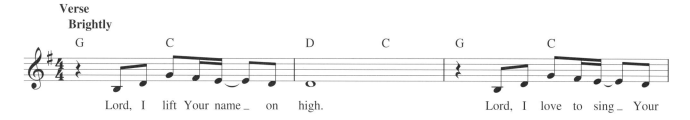

Verse
Brightly

Lord, I lift Your name _ on high. Lord, I love to sing _ Your

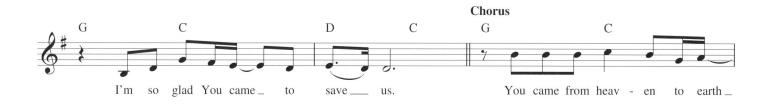

prais - es. I'm so glad You're in ____ my life.

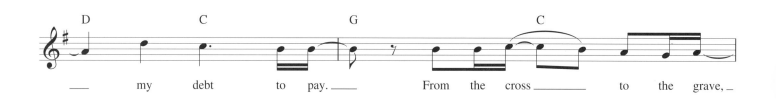

I'm so glad You came _ to save ____ us. **Chorus** You came from heav - en to earth _

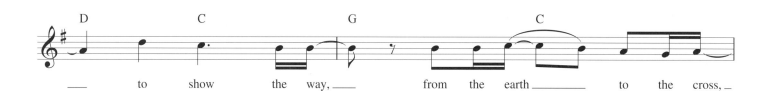

____ to show the way, ____ from the earth _____ to the cross, _

my debt to pay. ____ From the cross _____ to the grave, _

____ from the grave ____ to the sky; ____ Lord, I lift Your name _ on high.

Lord, Reign in Me

Words and Music by Brenton Brown

Additional Lyrics

2. Over ev'ry thought, over ev'ry word,
   May my life reflect the beauty of my Lord,
   'Cause You mean more to me than any earthly thing.
   So won't You reign in me again?

More Precious Than Silver

Words and Music by Lynn DeShazo

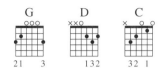

Lord, You are more pre - cious than sil - ver.

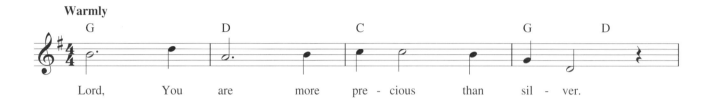

Lord, You are more cost - ly than

gold. Lord, You are more

beau - ti - ful ___ than dia - monds, and noth - ing I de -

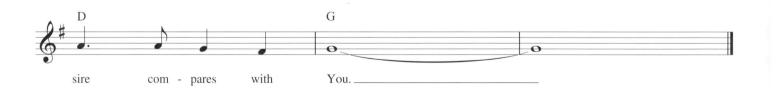

sire com - pares with You. ___

Seek Ye First

Words and Music by Karen Lafferty

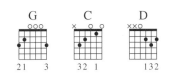

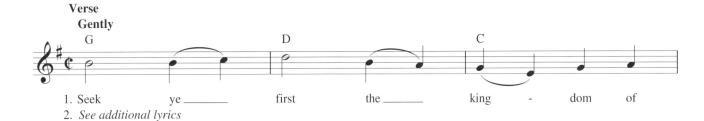

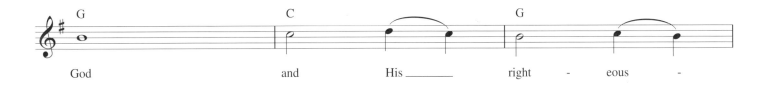

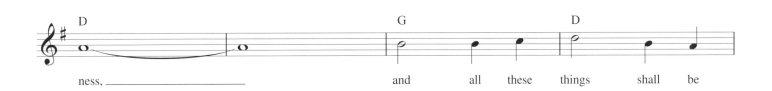

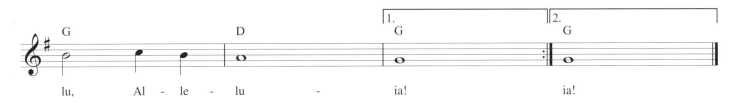

Additional Lyrics

2. Ask and it shall be given unto you,
   Seek and ye shall find,
   Knock and the door shall be opened unto you.
   Allelu, Alleluia!

My God Reigns

Words and Music by Darrell Evans

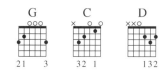

Verse
Moderately

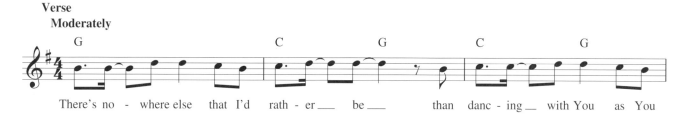

There's no - where else that I'd rath - er ___ be ___ than danc - ing ___ with You as You

sing o - ver me.   There's noth - ing else that I'd rath - er ___ do, ___ Lord, ___

___ than to wor - ship You. ___   So, re -

Verse

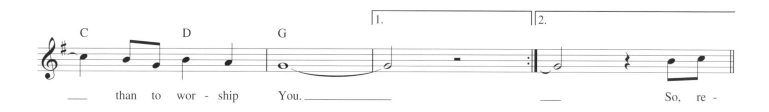

joice,   be glad,   re - joice, ___ O my soul,   for the Lord,   your God,   He
joice,   be glad,   your Fa - ther and your Friend   is the Lord,   your God,   whose

reigns for - ev - er - more.   I ___ re - joice, ___   for my God
rule will nev - er end.

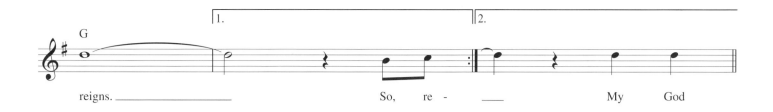

reigns. _____ So, re - ___ My God

Chorus

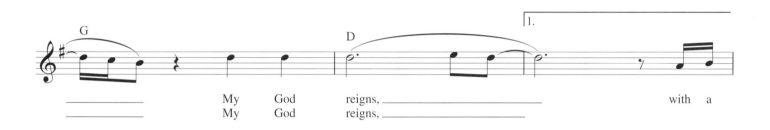

reigns, _____ and I dance the dance __ of praise. __
reigns, _____ and I wor - ship with - out shame. __

_____ My God reigns, _____ with a
_____ My God reigns, _____

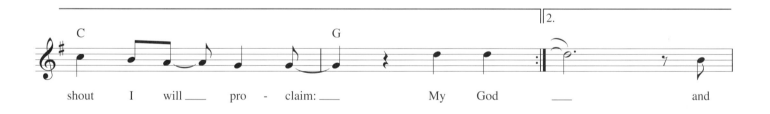

shout I will ___ pro - claim: ___ My God ___ and

I will ___ re - joice, for my God ___ reigns. _____

Step by Step

Words and Music by David Strasser "Beaker"

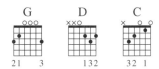

Moderately fast

Oh God, You are my _____ God, and

I will ev - er praise _ You. O God, You are my _____

God, and I will ev - er praise _ You. I will

seek You in the morn - ing, and I will

learn to walk in Your _ ways. _____ And step by step You'll lead _

_____ me, and I will fol - low You all of my _ days.

Take My Life
(Holiness)

Words and Music by Scott Underwood

Additional Lyrics

2. Faithfulness, faithfulness is what I long for.
Faithfulness is what I need.
Faithfulness, faithfulness is what You want from me.

3. Brokenness, brokenness is what I long for.
Brokenness is what I need.
Brokenness, brokenness is what You want from me.

There Is a Redeemer

Words and Music by Melody Green

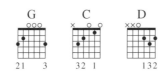

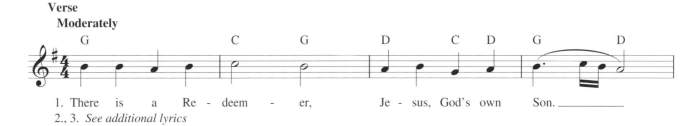

1. There is a Re- deem - er, Je - sus, God's own Son. _____
2., 3. *See additional lyrics*

Pre - cious Lamb of God, Mes - si - ah, Ho - ly

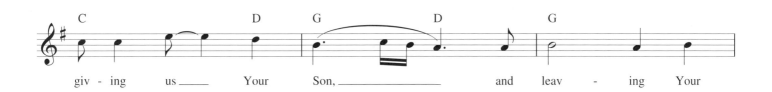

One.   Thank You, oh my Fa - ther, for

giv - ing us ___ Your Son, _____ and leav - ing Your

Spir - it till the work ___ on ___ earth is done.   done.

Additional Lyrics

2. Jesus, my Redeemer, name above all names.
Precious Lamb of God, Messiah, oh, for sinners slain.

3. When I stand in glory, I will see his face,
And there I'll serve my King forever in that holy place.

We Fall Down

Words and Music by Chris Tomlin

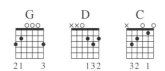

Verse
Worshipfully

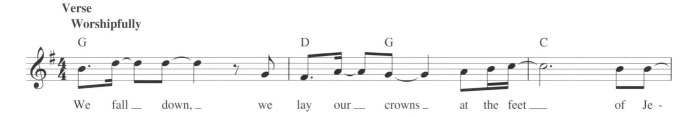

We fall down, we lay our crowns at the feet of Je-

-sus, the great-ness of mer-cy and love at the feet

of Je - sus. And we cry, "Ho-ly, ho-ly, ho-

Chorus

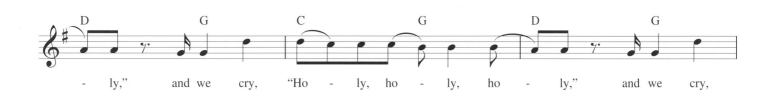

-ly," and we cry, "Ho-ly, ho-ly, ho-ly," and we cry,

"Ho-ly, ho-ly, ho-ly is the Lamb." _

1.   2.

You Alone

Words and Music by Jack Parker and David Crowder

Verse
Steadily, moving along

1., 3. You _____ are the on-ly _____ one I _____

2., 4. *See additional lyrics*

need. _____ I bow all of me _____ at Your _____

feet. _____ I wor-ship _____ You a -

lone. _____

Chorus

You _____ a - lone _____ are _____ Fa-ther, and You _____

a - lone _____ are _____ good.

You _____ a - lone _____ are _____ Sav-ior, and You _____

To Coda

a - lone _____ are _____ God. _____

Additional Lyrics

2., 4. You have given me more than I could ever have wanted,
And I want to give You my heart and my soul.

You Are My King

(Amazing Love)

Words and Music by Billy James Foote

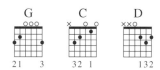

Verse
Moderately slow

1., 2. I'm for-giv-en be-cause You were _ for-sak-en.

I'm ac-cept-ed; You were _ con-demned. _

I'm a-live _ and well; _ Your Spir-it is _ with-in _ me be-

cause You died _ and rose _ a-gain. _

𝄋 Chorus

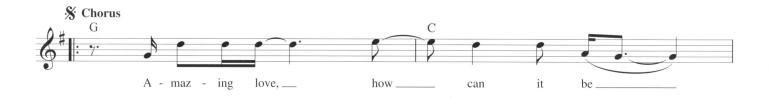

A-maz-ing love, _ how _ can it be _

that You, my _ King, _ would die _ for me? _

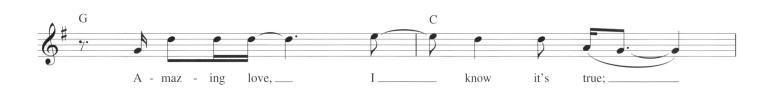

A - maz - ing love, ___ I _____ know it's true; _____

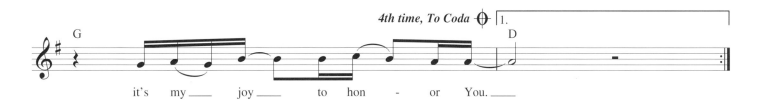

4th time, To Coda ⊕ | 1.

it's my ___ joy ___ to hon - or You. ___

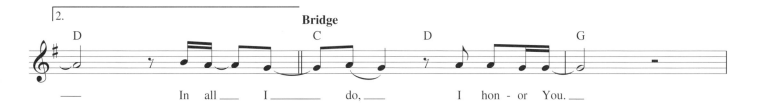

| 2.

Bridge

___ In all ___ I _____ do, ___ I hon - or You. ___

You are ___ my _____ King.

You are _____ my _____ King. Je - sus,

You are _____ my _____ King. Je - sus, You are ___ my ___

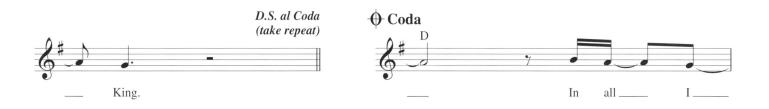

D.S. al Coda
(take repeat)

⊕ **Coda**

___ King.

___ In all ___ I _____

___ do, _____ I hon - or You. ___

Worthy, You Are Worthy

Words and Music by Don Moen

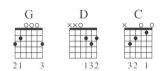

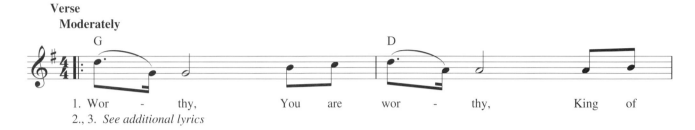

Verse
Moderately

1. Wor - thy, You are wor - thy, King of
2., 3. *See additional lyrics*

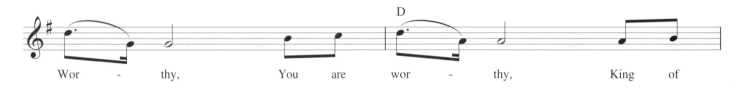

kings, Lord of lords, You are wor - thy.

Wor - thy, You are wor - thy, King of

kings, Lord of lords, I wor - ship You. You.

Additional Lyrics

2. Holy, You are holy,
   King of kings, Lord of lords,
   You are holy.
   Holy, You are holy,
   King of kings, Lord of lords,
   I worship You.

3. Jesus, You are Jesus,
   King of kings, Lord of lords,
   You are Jesus.
   Jesus, You are Jesus,
   King of kings, Lord of lords,
   I worship You.